Embracing Divine Purpose
Unraveling Purpose

A journey of faith and humanity, guided by divine light on the right path

CEULEMANS BRAGA

"In him we have obtained an inheritance, having been predestined according to the purpose of him who works all things according to the counsel of his will."
— Ephesians 1:11

Copyright Page

First Edition: 2025

ISBN:

Editorial Office: Website: Email:

Table of Contents

CHAPTER 1: SACRED ROOTS

"In him we have also obtained an inheritance, having been predestined according to the purpose of him who works all things according to the counsel of his will." - Ephesians 1:11 (Colossians 2:6-7)

The Seeds of Faith

In a humble family in Brazil, where dreams seemed distant and opportunities scarce, a child was born who would carry something extraordinary within him. There were no outward signs of greatness— no wealth, no privileged social position, no advanced formal education. But there was something much more powerful: the spiritual heritage passed down through generations of faith.

Ceulemans Braga's grandmother was a woman of prayer, one of those who know the secrets of the spiritual realm. Her hands, calloused from hard work, were the same ones that rose in intercession every morning. She did not know that she was planting prophetic seeds in her grandson's heart, seeds that would blossom years later in a foreign land.

"When you need something," she used to say to young Ceulemans, "if you are in danger, call on Jesus. Because He always hears our prayers." These seemingly simple words carried the weight of a divine revelation. The grandmother was not only teaching a prayer—she was prophesying about her grandson's spiritual destiny.

The Powerful Mix

Within young Ceulemans, a unique blend was forming: faith, dream, and achievement. It was a powerful combination that set him apart from other young men his age. While others were content with their present circumstances, he carried a holy restlessness, a sense that something greater was waiting for him.

This mixture was not the work of chance. It was the result of words planted with divine purpose, words that generated destinies. His grandmother, perhaps without fully understanding it, was being used by God to prepare an instrument that would serve many people in the future.

The family may have been humble in material resources, but they were rich in faith and determination. The young man learned early on that true wealth is not measured in possessions, but in the ability to dream, fight, and win. More importantly, he learned that there was a higher power guiding every step, every decision, every moment of his life.

The Divine Difference

In a world in the 21st century, where technology is advancing more and more, a question echoes in the human heart: "Who can we trust?" For Ceulemans, that answer was built from childhood through the example of a grandmother who trusted completely in the living God.

The word "trust" has a transformative power that can be positive or negative, depending on where it is placed. Ceulemans' grandmother taught him to place that trust in the right place: in
promises of God, in divine faithfulness, in the unconditional love of the Creator.

Regardless of where he was, Ceulemans stood out. Not because of arrogance or superiority, but because he carried within him an unshakeable conviction that God had a specific plan for his life. This conviction was the fuel that would propel him beyond the borders of his homeland.

The Promises That Sustain

The promises his grandmother spoke were not just words of comfort— they were prophetic decrees that would be fulfilled in due time. When she said that God had something special for her grandson, she was declaring a spiritual truth that would manifest in ways even she could not imagine.

These promises became anchors in Ceulemans' life. In moments of doubt, when the path seemed uncertain, he could return to his grandmother's words and find the strength to continue. It was as if each promise were a key that would open doors in the future.

The power of prophetic words is extraordinary. They don't just predict the future—they shape it. When a person of faith declares blessings over someone's life, those words take on a life of their own and work to fulfill themselves through the circumstances of life.

The Invisible Preparation

Without realizing it, Ceulemans was being prepared for a ministry that would transcend geographical and cultural boundaries. Every experience of his youth, every word of faith received, every moment of prayer witnessed in his grandmother's home—all of this was part of a divine curriculum that would equip him for what was to come.

God's preparation is rarely obvious at the time it happens. Often, it is only in hindsight that we can see how each piece fit perfectly into the divine puzzle. The humility of his family, his grandmother's faith, the financial difficulties, the dreams that seemed impossible—all of this was part of a larger plan.

God was shaping a vessel that would be used to bring hope, healing, and divine direction to people of different cultures and languages. Brazil was only the place of formation; the world would be his field of action.

The Eternal Foundation

The sacred roots planted in Ceulemans' childhood were not just family influence—they were eternal foundations that would sustain his entire spiritual journey. Faith not inherited, but cultivated; trust not based on circumstances, but on divine promises; purpose not invented, but revealed.

When the time came to leave his homeland, Ceulemans would not depart as an adventurer in search of fortune. He would leave as a man with a destiny, carrying within him the seeds of a ministry that would transform lives. The sacred roots that sustained him would ensure that, no matter how far he went, he would never lose his spiritual identity.

These roots would also serve as a source of wisdom and spiritual discernment. In moments when God spoke to his heart, he would recognize the voice because he had been trained since childhood to hear it. When he needed to minister to others, he would have a deep well of faith and spiritual experience from which to draw.

The Legacy That Transcends Generations

Ceulemans' grandmother may not have left significant material possessions, but she left something infinitely more valuable: a spiritual heritage that would be multiplied through the generations. Her prayers and prophetic words not only transformed her grandson's life, but through him would reach thousands of other people.

That is the beauty of spiritual sowing—it never stops bearing fruit. Words of faith spoken over a child can generate transformations that cross oceans and impact different cultures. The grandmother's spiritual investment in her grandson would become an investment in God's kingdom on a global scale.

Thus, the sacred roots planted in Brazilian soil would prepare to nourish a tree that would bear fruit on American soil, proving that God's purpose knows no boundaries and that His faithfulness reaches all generations who trust in His promises.

"These are the words that generate and transform destinies."

CHAPTER 2: THE JOURNEY BEGINS

"The purpose is greater than the calling" (Isaiah 41:10)

The Decision

December 2002. The suffocating heat of the Brazilian summer contrasted with the cold decision Ceulemans had made. At 21, he was about to leave everything behind and set off for an unknown country, where he knew no one and did not speak the language.

His grandmother held his hands with unusual strength. "Remember what I always told you," her voice trembled. "When you need something, if you are in danger, call on Jesus. He always hears our prayers."

Ceulemans nodded, feeling the weight of those words. They were not just advice—they were instructions for spiritual survival.

White Christmas

December 25, 2002. A day that should have been one of family celebration became the day of his departure. At just 21 years old and with a suitcase filled more with faith than belongings, Ceulemans boarded a plane to the United States.

When the plane landed and he left the airport, the shock was immediate: snow. Lots of snow. A white, pure place, covered by a frozen blanket.

"It was like I was dreaming," he recalled. "Just like the movies I watched on television. A wonderful place."

But the initial wonder soon gave way to harsh reality. Boston, Massachusetts—full of opportunities, but also immense challenges for a young Brazilian who could barely ask for water in English.

The First Steps

The first few weeks were a mixture of wonder and despair. No support network, no command of the language, no references. Only the faith his grandmother had instilled in him.

"I started working," he recalls. "Any job that came along, I took."

It was months of hard work, saving every dollar. While other young people went out to have fun, Ceulemans worked double shifts, carrying the vision of something greater.

The First Car

After months of saving money, Ceulemans finally bought his first car—a 1994 Toyota with 120,000 miles on it, costing
$3,500.

"My first car," he smiled proudly. "And I was so happy with it."

It was a symbol of progress, proof that the dream was not impossible. Excited, he decided to test his new acquisition. "I decided to take a drive around Boston."

It was around the time Garmin GPS was becoming popular. Ceulemans bought one and installed it in his car, feeling ready to explore his new city.

Lost

What started as a joyful outing quickly turned into an ordeal. "I filled up the tank and drove far away," he says.

American roads were different—wide, fast, with signs in English that he could barely decipher. The GPS seemed to confuse him more than help him.

"I was lost for two hours, not knowing where to go. I didn't speak English."

The sun was beginning to set. The gas tank was running low. Ceulemans, who had left Brazil with such confidence, now found himself completely lost.

"I started to get desperate," he admits.

The Divine Encounter

Unable to continue, Ceulemans stopped the car on the side of the road. His hands trembled on the steering wheel. The silence was deafening.

"I stopped the car and started talking to God."

It wasn't a formal prayer. It was the desperate cry of a lost young man, calling out to the God his grandmother had always told him was there.

And then it happened.

"His voice began to whisper in my heart."

It wasn't audible, but it was unmistakable—the Holy Spirit his grandmother had taught him to recognize.
"I started talking to Him about what to do." It wasn't a monologue of pleas, but a real dialogue.

Memories flowed. "I began to remember my grandmother, who always said that when I needed something, if I was in danger, I should cry out to Jesus. Because He always hears our prayers."

Those words now resonated with new power. "I remembered the origin of the word 'liberated'—the prophetic promises her grandmother had spoken over her life.

The Guidance

What happened was subtle but unmistakable. Mental clarity where before there had been confusion. Peace where before there had been panic.

Direction where before there had been disorientation.

Ceulemans felt clear impressions of which direction to take. It wasn't the GPS that guided him home—it was the gentle voice of the Holy Spirit.

He started the car, this time with steady hands and a calm heart. He followed his inner impressions, turning when he felt he should turn. And slowly, miraculously, the roads began to look familiar.

When he arrived home, it was already dark. He had left for a casual drive and returned from a transformative spiritual journey.

Lessons from the Road

That experience taught him some fundamental lessons:

Vulnerability creates space for the divine. It was when he stopped trying to figure things out on his own that he was able to hear God clearly.
Prophetic words are activated in times of need. His grandmother's wisdom was prophetic preparation.

Divine guidance is real and available for everyday situations. God cared about a young man lost in Boston.

Understanding Purpose

In the days that followed, Ceulemans began to understand something profound. Being lost and being guided wasn't just about finding his way home—it was about learning to trust divine guidance for his entire life.

"It took me a while to understand the source, that the purpose is greater than the calling."

The calling had been to come to America. But the purpose was to learn to live in constant communication with the Holy Spirit, developing spiritual sensitivity that would eventually enable him to help others when they were lost.

Each challenge—language, culture, loneliness, finances—was not an obstacle, but preparation. God was using immigration to mold him, to teach him to depend on divine guidance.

Sacred American Soil

Brazil had been where the seeds were planted. America was becoming the soil where they would germinate.

"Only 21 years old in a land blessed by God." It was no longer just Brazilian soil that was sacred—any place where God manifested himself became sacred ground.

That Toyota on the side of the road had become a temporary altar, a place of divine encounter as sacred as any church. It was where a young immigrant learned: God is not limited to designated holy places. He meets His children wherever they are.

The Beginning

Looking back, Ceulemans saw how that lost day in Boston was when he truly found his way. Not just back home, but to his spiritual destiny.

"In this journey of life, we realize that we are not the focus." The journey was never about personal success. It was about becoming an instrument through which God could manifest His love to others.

Every person he would eventually help would be a beneficiary of the lessons learned on that cold afternoon in Boston—lost but being found, desperate but being comforted, confused but being guided.

The journey had begun. And the purpose was always greater than the calling.

"God reminded me of my origins and His promises."

CHAPTER 3: THE LADY AT THE GROCERY STORE

"Put your foot where God is putting the road. You are not alone." (2 Corinthians 5:7)

The Divine Whisper

It was an ordinary afternoon like so many others when Ceulemans decided to do a little shopping at the local supermarket. There was nothing special about the day—just the routine need to buy a few items for the house. But God had other plans for that seemingly ordinary visit.

The moment he walked through the automatic doors of the store, something extraordinary happened. A voice began to speak within him—not an audible voice, but that characteristic whisper of the Holy Spirit that he had learned to recognize since childhood. It was the same voice that had guided him when he was lost in Boston with his first car, the same presence that always manifested itself in moments when God wanted to use him to touch someone's life.

The voice did not speak in specific words, but in clear impressions and unmistakable directions. It was as if the Holy Spirit was preparing him for something that was about to happen, alerting his spiritual senses to a divine opportunity that would present itself.

The First Encounter

Right at the entrance to the supermarket, his eyes were drawn to a woman of about 61 years of age. It was no coincidence
— Ceulemans had already learned that when God draws our attention to someone, there is always a specific reason. The Holy Spirit had spoken to his heart that something important was about to happen, and that woman was

part of the divine plan.

The woman walked slowly through the aisles, with the posture of someone carrying more than just a shopping cart. There was something in her eyes—a mixture of dignity and concern that touched Ceulemans' heart deeply. He watched her discreetly while doing his own shopping, feeling a growing certainty within himself that God was orchestrating this encounter.

Throughout his time walking the aisles of the supermarket, Ceulemans remained attentive to the whisperings of the Holy Spirit. It was as if he were in constant conversation with God, asking, "Lord, what do you want to show me?" This was his usual prayer in moments when he felt the divine presence moving around him.

The Revelation at the Checkout

The climax came when Ceulemans finished his shopping and headed to the checkout to pay. And who was in line in front of him? The same woman God had pointed out to him at the supermarket entrance. It was no coincidence—it was divine confirmation that something important was about to unfold.

As he watched the scene unfold, Ceulemans saw the woman's expression gradually change from hope to embarrassment, and then to resignation. When it was her turn to pay, the total amount of her purchases exceeded the money she had available. The
reality was painful: she did not have enough money to take everything she had put in her cart.

With the dignity of someone who had already faced many difficulties in life, the woman began to separate the items, deciding which ones were essential and which ones she would have to leave behind. It was a heartbreaking moment for any sensitive observer, but for Ceulemans it was much more than that—it was the moment God had orchestrated for a demonstration of His love and provision.

The Voice That Won't Be Silenced

At that crucial moment, the same voice that had whispered at the beginning of his visit to the supermarket spoke again, this time with more urgency: "Aren't you going to do anything?" The question echoed in his heart like a divine challenge, an invitation to be God's hands and feet in that situation.

Ceulemans had long ago learned not to hesitate when the Holy Spirit directed him to take specific action. Without thinking twice, he approached the cashier and said simply, "You can put it in the bag for her to take." They were simple words, but they were filled with divine love and genuine compassion.

The reaction was immediate and moving. The woman, who until then had been struggling to maintain her composure, was overcome with deep emotion. Her words were a spontaneous prayer: "Thank you, my God, thank you so much!" She had instantly recognized that this was not just human kindness—it was divine intervention in her hour of need.

Recognition of the Sacred

The cashier, who had witnessed the entire scene, was also deeply moved by what she had just witnessed. With tears in her eyes, she looked at Ceulemans and declared, "You are an angel of the Lord. The world needs people like you."

Those words penetrated deep into Ceulemans' heart, but not as a personal compliment. Rather, they served as confirmation that God was using his life to manifest His love in practical and tangible ways. His heart and mind immediately responded, "The glory belongs to God."

It was a moment of mutual recognition of the sacred manifesting itself in everyday life. The employee had correctly identified the source of that action—it was not ordinary human kindness, but divine love flowing through a heart obedient to God's voice.

The Tangible Presence

What happened next was extraordinary. The glory of God became palpable in the environment. It was as if heaven had descended on the supermarket, transforming that ordinary commercial space into sacred ground. Ceulemans could physically feel the divine presence enveloping the entire situation.

This phenomenon was not new to him. He had learned that when we act in obedience to divine direction, especially in moments of practical ministry, God's presence manifests itself in a special way. It was confirmation that he had been used as an instrument in the hands of the Most High.

The fullness of God was in his heart, a sense of completeness and purpose that only comes when we are aligned with the divine will. It was not personal pride, but rather the deep satisfaction of knowing that he had been obedient to God's call for that specific moment.

Lessons from the Supermarket

That experience at the supermarket taught several fundamental lessons about how God works in everyday life:

First lesson: God uses ordinary moments for extraordinary manifestations of His love. A simple trip to the supermarket turned into an opportunity to demonstrate divine provision.

Second lesson: Spiritual sensitivity is crucial to recognizing the opportunities God places in our path. If Ceulemans had not learned to listen to the voice of the Holy Spirit, he would have completely missed the chance to be used by God.

Third lesson: Immediate obedience to divine direction is essential. There is no room for hesitation or rationalization when God calls us to act on behalf of someone in need.

Fourth lesson: When we act as instruments of God, He receives all the glory,

13

and everyone involved recognizes that something supernatural has happened.

The Multiplied Impact

What happened at that supermarket did not end with the payment of the groceries. The impact of that act of obedience multiplied in several ways:

For the woman who benefited, it was a tangible demonstration that God knows her needs and has people willing to be His extended hands. Her faith was strengthened and her hope renewed.

For the cashier, it was a powerful testimony that there are still people guided by divine principles, willing to sacrifice themselves for the sake of strangers. Her perspective on human kindness and the reality of God was impacted.

For Ceulemans, it was further confirmation of his calling as an instrument in God's hands, preparing him for even greater ministries to come in his spiritual journey.

The Continuity of Ministry

Leaving the supermarket with his heart overflowing with God's presence, Ceulemans was ready for the next ministry opportunity the Lord would prepare. He had learned that when we are obedient in one situation, God often presents us with the next opportunity almost immediately.

And that is exactly what happened. Still in the supermarket parking lot, his eyes were drawn to a young man of about 17 who was collecting shopping carts—a scene that instantly transported him back to his own experiences of youth and humility.

Once again, the word of God came into his heart, preparing him for another divine encounter, another opportunity to sow words that generate and transform destinies.

"These are the words that generate and transform destinies. The power that

comes from above."

CHAPTER 4: THE YOUNG MAN WITH THE CART

"Words that generate and transform destinies" (Psalms 77:11-12)

The Second Encounter

The glory of God still hung in the air when Ceulemans left the supermarket. His heart overflowed with the divine presence that had manifested itself moments before when he helped the elderly lady pay for her groceries. It was as if his whole being was vibrating at a different spiritual frequency, attentive and sensitive to the movements of the Holy Spirit.

He had learned through his experiences that when we are obedient in one situation, God often presents us with the next opportunity almost immediately. The spiritual journey was not made up of isolated moments, but of a continuous sequence of divine encounters, each one preparing the way for the next.

And that is exactly what happened.

Awakened Memories

Still in the supermarket parking lot, walking toward his car, Ceulemans' eyes were drawn—not by chance, but by divine guidance—to a young man of about 17. The boy was collecting shopping carts that customers had left scattered around the parking lot, pushing them in long lines back to the store entrance.

The scene touched something deep within Ceulemans. It wasn't just sympathy or casual compassion—it was recognition. That image instantly transported him back to his own past, to the difficult days when he himself had done exactly the same job.

He remembered the scorching sun on his back, the fatigue in his arms as he

16

pushed dozens of carts, the humility of a job that many considered menial. He remembered the feeling of starting from scratch, doing whatever work was available, saving every penny to build something better.

"Picking up carts at the supermarket," he muttered to himself, memories flooding his mind. "I did just that."

The Familiar Voice

Once again, as had happened inside the supermarket, the voice of the Holy Spirit began to speak within him. It was not an audible voice that others could hear, but that characteristic whisper he had learned to recognize and obey.

"The word of God came to me again," he recalls.

It was a feeling he knew well—a mixture of urgency and clarity, a specific direction without specific words. It was as if God was saying, "Go to him. Talk to him. I have something for you to share."

Ceulemans didn't hesitate. He had learned that hesitation is the enemy of divine obedience. When God speaks, the time for action is now, not after we think about it, not after we plan what to say, but now.
He approached the young man, who was focused on his task, pushing a long line of intertwined carts.

The Encounter

"Excuse me," Ceulemans called out, causing the young man to stop and look at him with a mixture of curiosity and caution. It was unusual for customers to approach him for a conversation.

The boy was thin, with the tired look of someone who worked long hours. His clothes were simple, a little worn. There was something in his eyes—a mixture of resignation and hope, like someone who does what he has to do but still dreams of something more.

"I just wanted to tell you something," Ceulemans began, feeling the words flow not from his own mind, but from that deeper source of divine wisdom. "I've done exactly what you're doing now."

The young man looked surprised. He looked at Ceulemans—an older, well-dressed man, clearly in a different life situation—and found it hard to imagine that he had once pushed carts around parking lots.

Sharing the Story

"It's true," Ceulemans continued. "When I arrived in the United States, I started from absolute zero. I didn't speak English, I didn't know anyone, I had no references. I took whatever job came along, including collecting carts, just like you're doing now."

He saw interest light up in the young man's eyes. It was an instant connection—the bridge between someone who had been through something and someone who was going through it now.

"I started talking about where God had taken me and put me," Ceulemans recalls. "In a few words, but blessed words were spoken to that young man."

He talked about cold mornings pushing carts, about saving every dollar, about dreaming of something better while doing a job that many considered humiliating. But he also talked about how that job had taught him discipline, humility, and respect for hard work.

"This job you're doing," Ceulemans said, "doesn't define who you are. It only defines where you are right now. And where you are right now is only the beginning of your story, not the end."

The Prophetic Word

Then something extraordinary happened. The words coming out of

Ceulemans' mouth began to carry a different weight, an authority that did not come from himself. It was the Holy Spirit speaking through him, releasing prophetic words about that young man's future.

"God has a plan for your life," he said, and as he spoke, he felt the anointing of those words. "You won't stay here forever. This is your training, your preparation. God is shaping your character through this work."

The young man had now completely stopped working. The carts were forgotten. He was totally focused on every word Ceulemans said, like someone thirsty drinking water.

"You have a specific purpose," Ceulemans continued. "God has planted dreams in your heart—don't ignore those dreams. This work is honest and worthy, but it is not your final destination. Continue to work hard here, but also prepare yourself for what God has planned for you."

Tears of Hope

Tears began to stream down the young man's face. They were not tears of sadness, but of something deeper—recognition, renewed hope, a sense that someone saw his real value beyond the work he did.

"How did you know?" the young man asked, his voice trembling. "How did you know I was about to give up? That I was feeling trapped, with no future?"

Ceulemans smiled gently. "I didn't know. But God knew. He sent me to talk to you today."

The young man wiped his tears with the back of his hand. "I wake up every day wondering if it's worth continuing. My friends mock my work. My parents are disappointed. I was starting to believe that this was all I would ever achieve in life."

"That's a lie," Ceulemans said firmly. "Those are voices trying to destroy your destiny before it manifests itself. But today, God wants you to know the truth: you have value, you have purpose, and you have a future."

The Seed Planted

They talked for a few more minutes. Ceulemans shared more details of his own journey—the challenges, the moments of
doubt, but also the victories, and how each difficult step had prepared him for the next level.

"Keep your integrity," Ceulemans advised. "Do this work with excellence, even if no one is watching. God is watching. He is seeing your heart, your faithfulness in the little things. And when you are faithful in the little things, He will entrust you with greater things."

Before leaving, Ceulemans placed his hand on the young man's shoulder. "Remember what we talked about today. When things get tough, when negative voices try to convince you to give up, remember: God has a plan. You are not here by accident. You are in training."

The Impact of Words

As he walked back to his car, Ceulemans reflected on what had just happened. "I realized who was speaking. It wasn't me. It was God speaking through me."

This was one of the most profound lessons he had learned on his spiritual journey: when we become available vessels, God can use us to speak life and hope to hearts that need to hear exactly what we have to share.

"These are the words that generate and transform destinies," he thought. They were not elaborate words or prepared speeches. They were simple words, but charged with divine authority and genuine love. They were words that found fertile ground in a heart desperate for hope.

The young man in the parking lot had received much more than an encouraging conversation. He had received a prophetic word, a divine declaration about his worth and future that could sustain him through the difficult days ahead.

Lessons from the Parking Lot

That encounter in the parking lot taught several important lessons:

First: God uses our past to minister to the present of others. Every difficult experience we go through can become a bridge of empathy and credibility when we help others going through the same thing.

Second: Never underestimate the power of prophetic words spoken at the right time. A five-minute conversation can change the trajectory of an entire life.

Third: Obedience to the Holy Spirit's promptings requires readiness. Ceulemans could have ignored the impression, rationalized that he was busy, or assumed that someone else would talk to the young man. But he obeyed immediately.

Fourth: We must always be ready to be used by God. Ministry doesn't only happen in formal settings like churches. It happens in parking lots, supermarkets, streets—wherever people in need and obedient servants meet.

The Power of Words

That night, when he got home, Ceulemans prayed for the young man in the parking lot. He didn't know his name, had no way of following his progress, but trusted that the seeds planted would bear fruit in God's time.

He thought about how words have creative power. His grandmother's words had shaped his own life. The words he shared that day could be shaping that young man's future.

"Words that generate and transform destinies," he murmured again, grateful to have been used as a divine instrument once more.

And somewhere that night, a 17-year-old boy slept with renewed hope, dreaming not only of collecting carts, but of the destiny God had promised through an obedient stranger in a parking lot.

"The power that comes from above—words that generate and transform destinies."

CHAPTER 5: HEALING THROUGH FAITH

"Put your foot where God puts the road" (Matthew 11:5)

The Dream Trip

Traveling with his family to Disney. It was a dream that Ceulemans had carried for years—to be able to give his wife and son that magical experience that he himself had never had as a child. When they finally had the financial means, he and his wife decided to make that dream come true, inviting a family of friends to share the adventure.

"My family, my wife, and a family of friends decided to visit Disney," he recalls with a smile. "It was a dream to visit Disney."

It was more than just fun. It was a milestone, a tangible testimony to how God had prospered his life since those difficult days pushing grocery carts and getting lost on the roads of Boston. Now, years later, he could give his family memories that would last forever.

The Divine Impression

On the morning of the trip to the park, as they were getting ready to leave, Ceulemans felt that familiar impression—the soft whisper of the Holy Spirit that he had learned to recognize and obey over the years.

He glanced at his Bible on the table. The day promised to be hot, and carrying a Bible to an amusement park seemed impractical. But the impression lingered.

"Honey, it's really hot today," he said to his wife. "Do you think I should take the Bible?"

His wife, who had learned to trust her husband's spiritual impressions, replied without hesitation, "What is the Lord saying to your heart? If He is telling you to take it, take it."

Ceulemans nodded. "So I took the Bible, put it in my backpack, and we went."

The Feeling

From the moment they entered the park, Ceulemans sensed something different. It wasn't anxiety or fear—it was that heightened spiritual sensitivity he recognized from times when God was about to use him for something important.

"But right from the start, right at the entrance to the park, I found myself quiet, feeling like something was about to happen," he recalls.

While the family laughed and marveled at the attractions, while his son excitedly pulled his hand to see the rides, a part of Ceulemans remained spiritually alert. Not in a way that robbed him of his joy, but in a way that kept him attuned to the Holy Spirit.

The Critical Moment

After visiting a few attractions, his son asked to go to the bathroom. His wife, who knew the park better, showed him where it was.

"We waited. He was taking too long," Ceulemans recalls. "I said to her, 'Stay here, I'll go see what's going on.

He started walking toward the restroom, but before he even got there, he came across a scene that made his heart sink: a family in complete despair.

On the ground, lying on the hot concrete of the park, was a girl of about 11. Her parents—a man of about 45 and a woman of about 39—were kneeling beside her, screaming for help, their voices breaking in panic.

"The father was around 45 years old, the mother around 39, and their daughter was 11," Ceulemans describes. "They were both desperately screaming and crying, and I approached them."

The Voice of the Spirit

Instantly, the Holy Spirit began to speak to Ceulemans. These were not audible words, but that clear and unmistakable divine communication he knew so well.

"I came back not knowing what to do, and I started talking to the Holy Spirit, and He began to minister to my mind with His voice."

The message was clear: "Do something."

But do what? There were thousands of people passing through the park. Professional help was surely on its way. And there he was, in the middle of a crowd, being called to act in a medical emergency.

"What? My word?" Ceulemans questioned internally. "But I felt fear and insecurity."

It was understandable. They were in a public place, surrounded by strangers, dealing with an unconscious child. There was the fear of embarrassment, of rejection, of doing something wrong. But stronger than the fear was the certainty of divine direction.

Obedience

"I remember the word released," he recalls, referring to those prophetic promises his grandmother had spoken over his life
—that he would be used by God in extraordinary ways.

With slightly trembling hands, Ceulemans took the Bible out of his backpack. Now he understood why God had insisted that he bring it.

"And I took the Bible out of my backpack and began to pray without ceasing what the Holy Spirit was ministering to me."

He knelt down beside the desperate family. The parents looked at him with eyes full of tears and panic, but also with a glimmer of hope—any help was welcome at that terrible moment.

Ceulemans began to pray aloud, not memorized or formal prayers, but words that flowed directly from the Holy Spirit through him. He laid his hands on the girl, feeling divine authority that did not come from himself, but from the power that comes from above.

The Crowd and the Miracle

Around them, a crowd began to form. Thousands of people were passing through the park, and many stopped to see what was happening. Some took out their phones to call for help, others just watched in silence.

"And the people began to glorify the name of the Lord in that place," Ceulemans testifies.

Something supernatural was happening. The atmosphere changed. It wasn't just a man praying—it was the manifest presence of God descending upon that desperate situation.

Ceulemans continued to pray, declaring life over the girl, invoking the name of Jesus, exercising the spiritual authority that had been given to him. The minutes seemed like an eternity, but he didn't stop.

The Recovery

"Then something extraordinary happened," he recalls with reverence in his voice. "After a few minutes, the police officers and the girl arrived. Jesus had healed her. She had already recovered."

The girl who had been unconscious, motionless on the ground, began to move. Her eyes opened. Color returned to her face. She looked around, confused about what had happened, but clearly conscious and recovered.

When the paramedics and police arrived, they found not a medical emergency in progress, but a scene of celebration and worship. The girl was sitting up, alert, talking to her parents who embraced her with tears of relief and gratitude.

"I exalted the name of the Lord, the power of the word released, with a divine purpose," Ceulemans says.

The Witnesses

The police officers and firefighters who arrived at the scene saw something they could not explain in conventional medical terms. A child who minutes earlier had been unconscious was now completely recovered, with no need for hospitalization or medical intervention.

"And my wife was worried because she saw that I was holding the Bible up high," Ceulemans recalls. His wife, watching from a distance, had recognized what was happening—her husband was being used by God in a powerful and public way.

"And at the same time she was worried about our son," he continues. "But the voice of the Lord came first."

This was an important principle: when God calls, He becomes the priority. Even legitimate concerns for his own son had to wait while Ceulemans obeyed the call to minister to that family in crisis.

The Parents' Testimony

The girl's parents looked at Ceulemans with gratitude that transcended words. Their eyes, once filled with panic and despair, now shone with tears of joy and spiritual recognition.

"The girl's parents knelt down and began to thank Jesus," he testifies. "I said, 'Jesus wants your family to be His.'"

It was the perfect moment for evangelism. Hearts were open, defenses were down. They had just witnessed a miracle, and they were ready to hear about the God who performs miracles.

"'Today is an opportunity He is giving you,'" Ceulemans told the parents. It wasn't pressure or manipulation—it was a genuine invitation at the most receptive moment possible.

The Profound Lesson

That day at Disney taught several fundamental lessons about faith, obedience, and the power of God:

First: The importance of obeying spiritual impressions, even when they seem impractical. Bringing a Bible to an amusement park on a hot day seemed unnecessary, but it was divine preparation for what was to come.

Second: God puts us in position before the need arises. Ceulemans didn't seek out that situation—he was simply going to the bathroom. But God orchestrated his steps to be in the right place at the right time.

Third: Overcome fear and insecurity to obey God. It was scary to act publicly, risking embarrassment, but obedience overcame fear.

Fourth: "This shows us the sensitivity of hearing and discerning God's voice," Ceulemans reflects. It is not enough for God to speak—we need to be tuned in to hear and ready to obey.

The Lasting Impact

That day at Disney became more than a happy family memory. It became a powerful testimony to God's power working through obedient vessels. The story would be told and retold, strengthening the faith of all who heard it.

For the girl's family, it was the day God demonstrated His love in a tangible and powerful way. For the witnesses in the park, it was evidence that the supernatural still happens. For the police and firefighters, it was a reminder that there are things beyond natural explanation.

And for Ceulemans, it was further confirmation of his calling and purpose— to be an instrument through which God's power is manifested to bring healing, hope, and salvation.

"Healing through faith—the power that comes from above."

CHAPTER 6: THE RESTORED MARRIAGE

"God desires to restore what is broken" (James 5:16)

The Desperate Phone Call

It was a rainy afternoon when Ceulemans' phone rang. On the other end of the line, a female voice trembling with tears could barely form coherent sentences.

"Please," the woman pleaded between sobs. "They said you could help us. Our marriage is falling apart. I don't know what to do anymore."

Ceulemans recognized that tone—it was the desperation of someone who had tried everything and reached the end of their own resources. He had learned that these were the moments when God most liked to intervene, when human beings finally recognized that they needed help beyond themselves.

"Tell me what's going on," he said calmly, already beginning to pray silently for the Holy Spirit to give him wisdom.

The Story of Marcela and Roberto

Marcela and Roberto had been married for twelve years. What had begun as a passionate romance had turned into a cold and distant coexistence. They barely spoke to each other, slept in separate bedrooms
, and the only thing that still kept them under the same roof were their two young children.

"He doesn't love me anymore," Marcela cried on the phone. "He spends all his time at work, and when he's home, he's on the phone or watching television. We haven't talked in months. I feel invisible."

Ceulemans listened attentively, but as she spoke, the Holy Spirit began to whisper something different in his heart. There was more to the story than just a distant husband and a neglected wife.

"Can you come see me?" Ceulemans asked. "I'd like to talk to both of you together."

There was hesitation. "I don't know if he'll come. He doesn't believe in God, and he thinks couples therapy is a waste of time."

"Tell him it's not therapy," Ceulemans replied. "It's just a conversation. If he loves his children, he should at least try, shouldn't he?"

The Meeting

Three days later, Marcela and Roberto were sitting in Ceulemans' office. The tension between them was palpable—they sat at opposite ends of the couch, avoiding eye contact. Roberto had his arms crossed, the defensive posture of someone who was there against his will.

Ceulemans opened the conversation with a simple prayer, asking for wisdom and clarity. Roberto rolled his eyes but did not protest.
"Before we talk about the problems," Ceulemans began, "I would like each of you to tell me about when you first met. What was it like in the beginning?"

Marcela spoke first, and as she talked about the early days of their relationship, something changed in her expression. Her eyes sparkled with the memory of the joy she had felt.

Roberto, despite his initial resistance, couldn't help but smile a little when she mentioned the disastrous first date where he spilled coffee on himself trying to impress her.

"Do you remember that?" Marcela asked, surprised, looking at him for the first time since they arrived.

"Of course I remember," Roberto murmured. "It was the most embarrassing day of my life."

For a moment, the tension eased. But it soon returned when Ceulemans asked, "So what changed?"

The Revelation

As they talked, blaming each other, listing offenses and hurts accumulated over the years, Ceulemans prayed silently. And then, suddenly, the Holy Spirit showed him something that was not being said.

"Roberto," Ceulemans interrupted gently, "you're afraid of something, aren't you?"

Roberto stopped mid-sentence, his expression hardening. "What are you talking about?"

"You're not distant because you don't love your wife," Ceulemans continued, the words flowing not from his own wisdom but from divine revelation. "You're distant because you're afraid of losing her. Just like you lost your mother."

The silence that followed was deafening. Marcela stared at her husband with wide eyes. Roberto turned pale.

"How do you...?" Roberto began, but his voice failed him.

"Your mother died when you were a teenager," Ceulemans said gently. "And you vowed never to get attached to anyone that way again, never to feel that pain again. So you pull away emotionally, keeping your distance, thinking you're protecting yourself."

Tears began to roll down Roberto's face—the first sign of real emotion he had shown. "I didn't... I didn't realize I was doing that."

The Root Wound

Ceulemans turned to Marcela. "And you, Marcela. You're not just sad because your husband is distant. You're furious."

Marcela blinked, surprised by the accuracy of the observation. "I have a right to be furious. He completely ignores me."

"Yes, but your anger comes from a deeper place," Ceulemans continued. "It comes from when your father abandoned your family when you were eight years old. You promised yourself you would never let a man make you feel worthless again. So when Roberto pulls away, it's not just about him—it's as if your father is rejecting you all over again."

Marcela covered her face with her hands, sobbing. "How do you know these things? I've never told anyone."

"I don't know," Ceulemans replied honestly. "But God knows. And He wants you to see that you're fighting against wounds from the past, not each other."

Understanding

For the first time in years, Roberto and Marcela truly looked at each other. Not with anger or resentment, but with understanding and compassion.

"I didn't know," Roberto said, his voice hoarse with emotion. "I didn't know I was making you feel the way your father did. I... I was just so afraid."

"And I didn't know you were afraid," Marcela replied, reaching hesitantly toward her husband. "I thought you just didn't care anymore."

"Do you see?" Ceulemans said softly. "Your enemy is not each other. The enemy is these unhealed wounds from the past that are controlling how you

33

react in the present."

He opened his Bible. "God doesn't just want to fix your marriage. He wants to heal the wounds that are destroying your marriage."

The Healing Process

In the weeks that followed, Ceulemans met regularly with Roberto and Marcela. Each session involved prayer, honest conversation, and working through the layers of pain and protection that both had built up.

For Roberto, it meant learning to recognize his patterns of avoidance and consciously choosing to connect, even when fear arose. It meant crying for the mother he had never allowed himself to properly mourn.

For Marcela, it meant forgiving not only Roberto, but also her father. It meant breaking the belief that she was worthless and embracing her identity as a beloved child of God.

"Forgiveness doesn't mean that what happened was okay," Ceulemans explained. "It means you are choosing not to let the pain of the past destroy your future."

It was a difficult process. There were times when they wanted to give up, when old wounds were touched and the instinctive reaction was to retreat or attack. But each time, they chose to stay, work through the pain, and trust the process.

The Transformation

Three months later, Roberto and Marcela returned for a visit. But this time, they walked in hand in hand. The tension was gone, replaced by a visible connection.

"We wanted to thank you," Marcela said, her eyes shining—but this time with joy, not tears of pain. "You saved our marriage."

"It wasn't me," Ceulemans gently corrected. "It was God. He simply used me to show you what you needed to see."

Roberto, the man who had first come with resistance and skepticism, spoke up: "I never believed in God. But what happened here... there's no natural explanation for how you knew those things about our past. And there's no explanation for the peace I feel now."

"God was waiting for you to recognize your need for Him," Ceulemans smiled. "He used the crisis in your marriage to bring you to Him."

"Now I understand," Roberto said. "It wasn't just about saving our marriage. It was about finding ourselves—finding God, finding healing, finding our true selves."

The Greater Lesson

That experience taught several profound lessons about relationships and restoration:

First: The visible problems in a relationship are often symptoms of deeper, invisible wounds. Treating only the symptoms never brings lasting healing.

Second: God can reveal hidden things that no conventional therapy would uncover. He sees not only the actions, but the hearts and the roots of the wounds.

Third: Real restoration requires facing pain, not avoiding it. It is in the process of acknowledging and working through wounds that healing happens.

Fourth: God often uses crises to bring us to the point where we finally seek Him. What appears to be an ending may actually be a new beginning.

The Living Testimony

Months later, Ceulemans met Roberto and Marcela at a church event— yes, church. The man who didn't believe in God was now sitting in the second row, Bible in hand, learning eagerly.

"Our children are different too," Marcela shared. "They feel the change in our home. There is no more tension, no more fighting. There is peace."

"And that," Ceulemans thought as he watched them leave, "is the power of divine restoration. It doesn't just fix what's broken—it transforms it into something stronger than it was before."

The marriage that was days away from ending in divorce was now a living testimony to God's power to restore, redeem, and renew. It was proof that nothing is too broken for God to fix.

"God doesn't just fix—He restores and transforms."

CHAPTER 7: CAREER DIRECTION

"God has specific plans for each person's work" (Proverbs 3:5-6)

The Woman in the Café

Ceulemans was sitting in a local café, reviewing some notes, when he noticed a woman at a nearby table. She was surrounded by papers, her laptop open, but her hands covered her face in a gesture of complete exhaustion.

He tried to return to his work, but the familiar impression from the Holy Spirit began to grow. "Go talk to her," the inner whisper was clear.

Ceulemans hesitated. She was a stranger in a public space. But he had learned to recognize when God was directing his steps.

"Excuse me," he said softly, approaching her. "Sorry to bother you, but... are you okay?"

The woman lifted her face, revealing red, tear-filled eyes. For a moment, she seemed to consider politely dismissing him. But then, as if a dam had broken, she began to speak.

"No," she admitted. "I'm not okay."

Patricia's Story

Her name was Patricia, 34 years old, with a degree in engineering and a master's in business administration. On paper, she was successful—a senior manager at
a large technology company, six-figure salary, office with a view.

"But I wake up every morning with a weight on my chest," she confessed. "I go to work and feel like I'm slowly dying inside. Every meeting, every report, every day is torture."

Ceulemans listened as she poured out years of frustration. She had followed the "right" path—the best schools, the best jobs, the career progression that everyone envied. But somewhere along the way, she had completely lost herself.

"My parents are proud. My friends think I have the perfect life. But I feel empty," she said. "And the worst part is, I don't know what I really want to do. I just know it's not this."

The Divine Question

As Patricia spoke, Ceulemans prayed silently. And then, the Holy Spirit gave him a specific question to ask.

"Patricia, what did you love to do when you were a child? Before anyone told you what you should be?"

She blinked, surprised by the question. "I... I don't know. It's been so long..."

"Think," Ceulemans encouraged her. "What kind of child were you? What made you lose track of time?"

Slowly, memories began to surface. "I drew," she said, almost shyly. "I spent hours drawing. I created stories,
characters, entire worlds. My school notebooks were full of drawings in the margins."

"And what happened to that?"

"My parents said art wasn't a real career," she replied, the old pain visible in her voice. "That I needed to be practical, study something that would make money. So I stopped drawing."

The Revelation

"You didn't stop drawing," Ceulemans gently corrected her. "You buried a part of yourself. And now that part is suffocating, and you feel it as this weight on your chest."

Tears began to stream down Patricia's face. "But I can't just drop everything and become an artist. I have bills to pay, responsibilities. It would be irresponsible."

"No one is telling you to drop everything tomorrow," Ceulemans said. "But you need to understand something important: God gave you those talents and passions for a reason. When you ignore them completely, you are rejecting part of His purpose for your life."

He continued, "You're living someone else's dream—probably your parents' dream for you. But it's not your dream, and it's definitely not what God planned."

The Specific Guidance

As they talked, the Holy Spirit began to give Ceulemans specific insights about Patricia's path.

"You have unique skills," he said. "You understand technology and business, but you also have artistic creativity. That's not common. Have you considered user experience design? Product design? Areas where art and technology meet?"

Patricia's eyes widened. "I... I never thought of it that way."

"God wastes nothing," Ceulemans explained. "All those years in technology were not a mistake. They were preparation. But you need to integrate all the parts of who you are, not just the part your parents approved of."

He felt the Holy Spirit directing his next words. "In the next three months, you will receive an offer. It will seem scary because it will be different from what you know. But it will be the beginning of the right path."

The Discovery Process

Patricia began meeting with Ceulemans regularly. Each meeting involved prayer, honest conversations about her fears and dreams, and practical steps to rediscover her creativity.

She began drawing again, at first just for herself. It was strange and uncomfortable at first—like using a muscle that hadn't been exercised in years. But slowly, something inside her began to awaken.

"It's like breathing again," she said at one of their meetings. "I didn't realize how suffocated I was until I started drawing again."

But there was still fear. "What if I fail? What if I'm not good enough? What if my parents are right that art isn't a real career?"

"You're asking the wrong questions," Ceulemans replied. "The right question isn't 'What if I fail?' It's 'What if I die without ever trying?' What kind of life is that?"

The Offer

Exactly two and a half months later, Patricia received a message on LinkedIn. A tech startup was looking for someone to lead its design department— someone who understood both technology and creativity.

"It's half my current salary," she told Ceulemans, her voice trembling between fear and excitement. "But it would be real creative work. Design, art direction, building experiences for users."

"And what is your heart saying?" Ceulemans asked.

"My heart is saying yes. But my head is screaming about financial security and what people will think."

"Remember what I said about an offer in three months?"

Patricia nodded, her eyes widening. "You said... you said exactly three months. How did you know?"

"I didn't know," Ceulemans smiled. "But God knew. He was preparing this for you even before you asked."

The Decision

The decision wasn't easy. Patricia's parents were horrified when she told them. "Are you going to throw away your career on a whim?" her mother cried. "All that education, wasted!"

Friends questioned her sanity. "You're having a midlife crisis," some said. "Don't do anything rash."

But every night when Patricia prayed, she felt the same peace about the decision. And she remembered Ceulemans' words: "When you are aligned with God's purpose, there is peace, even when there is fear."

She accepted the offer.

The Transformation

Six months later, Patricia returned to visit Ceulemans. But she was a different person—literally glowing, with an energy and life that hadn't been there before.

"I woke up today excited to go to work," she said, laughing. "Can you believe it? For the first time in years, I actually wanted to go to work."

The lower salary had required adjustments. She had moved to a smaller apartment and cut unnecessary expenses. But the change was worth every penny.

"My job isn't just a job now," she explained. "It's expression. It's purpose. Every project is an opportunity to create something that makes a difference in people's lives."

And there was more. "The company is growing rapidly. My boss hinted that if we continue at this pace, they will promote me to

creative director next year. With a salary that will exceed what I earned at my previous job."

"But even if that doesn't happen," she quickly added, "I wouldn't go back. Because for the first time, I am truly myself."

The Unexpected Testimony

Most surprising was the impact on her family. Her parents, who were initially horrified, began to see the change in her.

"My mom called me last week," Patricia shared. "She cried and apologized for forcing me to bury my creativity. She said she now sees how I was dying inside at my other job."

Even her former coworkers noticed. "Some of them reached out to me," she said. "They said my change inspired them to question whether they are on the right path. One colleague just signed up for night classes in photography."

The Profound Lesson

That experience taught several important truths about calling and purpose:

First: Success in the eyes of the world does not mean alignment with God's purpose. You may be at the top of a ladder leaning against the wrong wall.

Second: God does not waste our experiences. Even detours can be part of the preparation for where He is leading us.

Third: It's never too late to realign your life with your true calling. The question is not how long you've been on the wrong path, but how long you will continue on it.

Fourth: When you follow God's purpose, He provides. Provision may not come in the way we expect, but it comes.

The Domino Effect

A year later, Patricia was not only thriving in her career—she was helping others find their paths as well.

She started a mentoring group for creative professionals, especially those transitioning from traditional corporate careers. "I want to be to them what you were to me," she told Ceulemans.

And the cycle continued. Each person Patricia helped became a source of light for others, creating waves of transformation that spread far beyond their original meeting in a coffee shop.

"See?" Ceulemans thought, watching it all unfold. "When a person finds their true purpose, it's never just about them. It's about all the lives they will touch when they finally become who they were created to be."

"Your work is worship when it is aligned with your divine purpose."

CHAPTER 8: FREEDOM FROM ADDICTIONS

"No one is beyond God's redemptive power" (John 8:32)

The Early Morning Call

The phone rang at three in the morning. Ceulemans woke up immediately, her heart already racing before she even answered. Calls at this hour rarely brought good news.

"Hello?" His voice was hoarse with sleep.

"Ceulemans?" It was a male voice, trembling, desperate. "Do you remember me? I'm Carlos. You helped my sister a few months ago..."

"Carlos, yes, I remember. What happened?"

"I need help." The voice broke. "I... I can't take it anymore. If I don't get help now, I'm going to die. I know it."

Ceulemans was wide awake now. "Where are you?"

"In a motel. I just used again and... something inside me broke. I called you because I had no one else."

"Give me the address," Ceulemans said, already getting up. "I'm on my way."

The Encounter

Thirty minutes later, Ceulemans knocked on the door of the cheap motel room. Carlos opened it, and what Ceulemans saw shocked him. The man in front of him
was unrecognizable—too thin, sunken eyes, visibly shaking.

44

Carlos was 28, but he looked 50. His arms were covered in needle marks. The room reeked of alcohol and despair.

"Thanks for coming," Carlos said, collapsing into a chair. "I know it's three in the morning. I just... I didn't know who else to call."

"Tell me your story," Ceulemans said gently, sitting down.

The Descent

Carlos had started drinking at age 15, just to fit in with his friends. Then came marijuana, then harder drugs. By age 20, he was addicted to heroin.

"I lost everything," he said, the words pouring out in a desperate stream. "I lost my job, my fiancée left me, my family won't talk to me anymore. My mother cries every time she sees me. My father said I'm no longer his son."

He had tried to quit several times. Rehab, therapy, support groups. "But I always come back," he confessed. "It's like something pulls me back. No matter how strong I am, no matter how much I want to quit, I always come back."

"Today was the last straw," Carlos continued, tears now streaming freely. "I stole money from my sister—the only person who still talks to me. She has two small children, and I stole her rent money. What kind of person does that?"

The Spiritual Revelation

As Carlos spoke, Ceulemans saw more than just an addict. He saw something deeper—spiritual bonds, invisible chains that kept Carlos trapped beyond his chemical dependency.

"Carlos," Ceulemans said gently, "you know this isn't just about drugs, right?"

Carlos looked at him confused. "What are you talking about?"

"You're trying to fill a void inside you. And every time you use, that void just gets bigger."

"Of course there's a void," Carlos said bitterly. "That's what addicts do— we try to fill the void."

"But where does that emptiness come from?" Ceulemans asked. "When did it start?"

Carlos was silent for a long moment. Then, in a low voice: "When my older brother died. I was 14. He was
16. It was a car accident. He was my hero, my best friend."

"And you never processed that loss," Ceulemans said. "So you started using to not feel the pain."

"It's more than that," Ceulemans continued, the words coming as if from divine revelation. "You carry guilt. You think it should have been you in the accident, not him."

Carlos turned pale. "How did you...? I've never told anyone that. But yes. My brother was the good one. Smart, athletic, loved by everyone. I was the problem child. It should have been me."

The Spiritual Battle

"The enemy has been using that guilt to destroy you," Ceulemans explained. "You've been punishing yourself for 14 years. Every time you use, it's a little more self-punishment. You don't think you deserve to be clean, so you always find an excuse to go back."

"But there's also something else," Ceulemans said. "There are spiritual ties here. You opened doors through drugs, and entities found a place to dwell."

This sounded strange to Carlos, but somehow it resonated as truth. "What do I do?"

46

"First, you need to forgive yourself," Ceulemans said. "Your brother's death wasn't your fault. It wasn't your choice. And he wouldn't want to see you destroying yourself in his memory."

Then Ceulemans opened his Bible. "Second, we need to break these spiritual chains. Are you willing to give your life to Jesus Christ?"

Carlos hesitated. "I don't know if I believe in God. And if I do, I'm sure He wants nothing to do with me after everything I've done."

"That's exactly the thinking that's keeping you trapped," Ceulemans said. "The truth is, God has never stopped wanting you. No matter how far you've gone, He's waiting for you to come back."

The Prayer of Deliverance

In the hours that followed, Ceulemans prayed for Carlos. These were not gentle, comforting prayers—they were prayers of spiritual warfare, confronting the forces that held Carlos captive.

"In the name of Jesus," Ceulemans declared, "I break the chains of addiction that bind Carlos. I cast out every spirit of bondage, guilt, and self- destruction. Carlos is free!"

Carlos began to cry—not soft tears, but deep, convulsive sobs that came from a place beyond the physical. It was as if something was being torn from him, layers of pain and darkness being removed.

"Forgive yourself," Ceulemans encouraged him. "Say out loud, 'I forgive myself for my brother's death, which was not my fault.'"

At first, Carlos couldn't do it. The words stuck in his throat. But finally, in a broken whisper: "I forgive myself. It wasn't my fault."

"Louder," Ceulemans insisted.

"I FORGIVE MYSELF!" Carlos shouted, years of guilt finally breaking. "IT

WASN'T MY FAULT!"

Dawn

When the sun rose, something had changed. Carlos was still shaking from physical withdrawal, still looked exhausted. But there was something different in his eyes—a glimmer of hope where before there had been only despair.

"What happened?" Carlos asked, confused. "I feel... lightness. As if a weight I've been carrying for years has simply disappeared."

"You have been set free," Ceulemans said simply. "Spiritually, the chains have been broken. But now comes the hard part—the physical and emotional process of recovery."

Ceulemans helped Carlos enter a Christian rehabilitation program. "The spiritual battle has been won," he explained, "but you still need practical support. Recovery is a journey, not a single event."

The Process

The first few months were brutally difficult. The physical withdrawal was agonizing. There were moments when Carlos wanted to give up, when the old voices whispered that it would be easier to just use one more time.

But something was different this time. Where before he always ended up giving in, now he had the strength to resist. The overwhelming guilt that always pulled him back was truly broken.

"I still have cravings," he admitted to Ceulemans during a visit. "But I don't have the compulsion. Before, it was as if something controlled me. Now, I have real choice."

He began attending recovery meetings and rebuilding bridges with his family. His mother cried when he showed up at her door, three months sober, asking for forgiveness.

"I have my son back," she said, hugging him as if she would never let go.

The Restoration

A year later, Carlos was unrecognizable—but this time in a good way. He had gained healthy weight, his eyes sparkled with life, his skin no longer had that gray, deathly appearance.

He had gotten a job, started paying his sister back, and was rebuilding his life step by step. But more importantly, he had found purpose.

"I started volunteering at the rehab center," he told Ceulemans. "Helping other addicts. Because I know what it's like to be in that dark place with no hope."

He paused, emotion in his voice. "And I can tell them what you told me— that no matter how far they've gone, no matter what they've done, they're not beyond God's reach."

The Living Testimony

Carlos became living proof of God's power to set people free. People who knew him before could hardly believe the transformation.

"I was dead," he often testified. "Not just dying—I was dead inside. And God raised me up. There's no other explanation."

He eventually returned to school and studied to become an addiction counselor. "I want to spend my life helping others find the freedom I found," he said.

And his family? His mother said she had received two miracles in her life— the birth of Carlos and his rebirth.

The Profound Lesson

Carlos' story taught important truths about addiction and freedom:

First: Addiction is rarely just about the substance. There are deeper emotional and spiritual wounds that need to be healed.

Second: Spiritual battles require spiritual solutions. Therapy and support are important, but some cases need direct spiritual intervention.

Third: No one is too far gone. No matter how deep someone has fallen, God can reach them and restore them.

Fourth: Deliverance is both instantaneous and processual. The moment of spiritual breakthrough can happen overnight, but full recovery is a journey that requires time and ongoing support.

The Cascade Effect

Years later, Carlos was leading his own recovery ministry. Dozens of people had found deliverance through his testimony and help.

"That phone call at three in the morning," he often said, "was the moment I chose life over death. And Ceulemans answered. He could have ignored the phone. But he came. And that made all the difference."

And with every person Carlos helped find freedom, the impact of that night in a cheap motel continued to multiply—proof
that God's redemption has no limits and His power to restore knows no boundaries.

"From the depths of addiction to the light of freedom—the redemptive power of God."

CHAPTER 9: DIVINE PROTECTION

"The protective hand of God over His people" (Psalms 91:7)

The Night Warning

Ceulemans woke up suddenly at 2:30 in the morning. It wasn't a noise that woke him, nor was it a nightmare. It was something deeper—a spiritual urgency that instantly roused him from sleep.

He knew this feeling. It was the Holy Spirit awakening him to pray.

Sitting up in bed, he began to pray, but he didn't know exactly what for. He just had a strong impression about his neighbor, Miguel—a man he barely knew, who just waved politely when they passed each other.

"Lord, what's going on?" Ceulemans prayed. "Why am I thinking about Miguel?"

The answer came not in words, but in a growing urgency. Something was wrong. Something was about to happen.

The Urgent Feeling

Ceulemans got up and went to the window. Everything looked normal on the quiet street. Miguel's house was dark, apparently everyone was asleep.

But the impression did not diminish. On the contrary, it grew stronger. "Go there," the inner whisper was clear. "Now."

Ceulemans hesitated. It was almost three in the morning. He barely knew Miguel. What would he say? "Sorry to bother you in the middle of the night, but God told me to come here"? It would sound absurd.

But he had learned not to question these impressions. He got dressed quickly and crossed the street.

The Discovery

When he reached Miguel's door, something stopped him from knocking right away. Instead, he walked around the house. And that's when he saw it—a faint light coming from the basement, visible through a small window.

As he approached, Ceulemans smelled something strange. Gas.

His heart raced. Without thinking, he ran to the front door and began knocking loudly. "MIGUEL! MIGUEL! WAKE UP!"

It took almost a minute—which seemed like an eternity—before lights came on inside the house. Miguel appeared at the door, confused and irritated.

"Oh my God...? It's three in the morning!"

"You have a gas leak," Ceulemans said quickly. "I can smell it from here. You need to get out of the house now and call the fire department."

The Critical Situation

Miguel was about to argue when he smelled it himself. His expression instantly changed from irritation to alarm.

"My wife. My children," he said, turning quickly. "EVERYONE, GET OUT OF THE HOUSE NOW!"

The next few minutes were controlled chaos. Miguel woke his wife and three children, and they all quickly left the house. The neighbors began to wake up with the commotion. Someone called the fire department.

When the firefighters arrived and inspected the house, their expressions were grave. "You were very lucky," the captain said. "The heater in the basement malfunctioned. The gas concentration was close to explosive levels. If someone had turned on a light or used the stove in the morning..."

He didn't need to finish the sentence. Everyone understood. The entire family could have died—either from the explosion or from carbon monoxide poisoning while they slept.

The Question

After the firefighters had resolved the situation and declared the house safe, Miguel approached Ceulemans. The sun was beginning to rise.

"How did you know?" he asked. "How did you know there was a leak? You couldn't have smelled it from across the street."

Ceulemans smiled gently. "I didn't know. But God knew. He woke me up and told me to come check your house."

Miguel looked at him skeptically. "Are you saying that God woke you up in the middle of the night to save my family?"

"Yes," Ceulemans replied simply. "Exactly that."

Resistance and Revelation

Miguel was a practical businessman who had no time for religion. "I don't believe in God," he said bluntly. "It must have been a coincidence. Or maybe you heard the heater making noise."

"Miguel," Ceulemans said patiently, "do you really think it was coincidence that I woke up at exactly that moment, felt an urgency specifically about you, and came to check your house at such a specific time?"

Miguel's wife, Ana, who was listening to the conversation, had tears in her eyes. "It wasn't coincidence," she said softly. "It was a miracle."

She turned to her husband. "Miguel, our children could have died tonight. We all could have died. And this man, whom we barely know, was awakened by something to save us. How can you call that a coincidence?"

The Conversation

In the days that followed, Miguel couldn't stop thinking about the incident. He was a logical man who always had rational explanations for everything. But this... this defied his logic.

A week later, he knocked on Ceulemans' door.

"Do you have a few minutes to talk?" Miguel asked, visibly uncomfortable. They sat down in Ceulemans' backyard. Miguel was restless, struggling to find words.

"I can't stop thinking about that night," he finally said. "I've tried to find rational explanations. That maybe you have insomnia and were awake anyway. That maybe you heard something. But nothing makes sense."

He paused. "The truth is, you had no natural reason to be at my house at that hour. And if you hadn't come..."

His voice broke. "My children. They're 6, 8, and 10 years old. They could have been killed."

The Explanation

"God loves your family," Ceulemans said gently. "Even if you don't believe in Him, He believes in you. He has plans for you, for Ana, for your children."

"Why would He save someone who doesn't even believe in Him?" Miguel asked.

"Because God's love is not conditional," Ceulemans explained. "He doesn't expect you to deserve Him. He simply loves. And that night, He chose to use an obedient neighbor to protect your family."

Miguel was silent for a long moment. "What if you hadn't obeyed? What if you had decided it was too late or too strange?"

"But I did obey," Ceulemans replied. "And that's the beauty of the partnership between God and willing people. He directs us, we obey, and miracles happen."

The Transformation

That conversation was the beginning of a transformation in Miguel. He began to ask questions—about God, about faith, about purpose and meaning.

"I always thought faith was for weak people," he admitted. "People who needed emotional crutches. But you're not weak. You woke up in the middle of the night, crossed the street based on nothing more than a feeling, risked looking crazy. That's not weakness."

"Faith isn't weakness," Ceulemans agreed. "It's strength to obey even when it doesn't make logical sense. It's trust that there is a wisdom greater than our own."

Miguel began attending church with Ceulemans. Ana, who had always been a believer but a silent practitioner so as not to conflict with her husband, was overjoyed.

"I prayed for 15 years for my husband to know God," she told Ceulemans, crying with gratitude. "And God used a gas leak to answer my prayer."

The Impact on the Family

The change in Miguel impacted the entire family. His children, who had never had any religious education, began asking questions about God.

"Daddy," his 8-year-old daughter asked, "Mr. Ceulemans said that God woke you up to save us. Does God really do that?"

Miguel, who months earlier would have said they were just stories, now replied, "Yes, my dear. God does that. And He did it for us."

The family began to pray before meals, something Ana had always wanted but never insisted on. Miguel read Bible stories to the children before bedtime, still stumbling over the words, still learning, but trying.

Continued Protection

Three months after the incident, Miguel returned to visit Ceulemans with an extraordinary story.

"You won't believe what happened," he said, still processing it. "I was driving on the highway yesterday. Heavy rain, poor visibility. Suddenly, I had a very strong impression—'Change lanes. Now.'"

"And you obeyed?" Ceulemans asked, already knowing the answer.

"Yes. It didn't make sense—the lane next to me was slower. But after that night with the gas, I learned to listen to these impressions. So I changed lanes."

"Five seconds later, a truck lost control and crashed exactly where I had been. If I had still been in that lane..." He didn't need to finish.

"You are learning to listen to God's voice," Ceulemans smiled. "He didn't stop protecting you that night. He continues to do so."

The Profound Lesson

Miguel's story taught several truths about divine protection:

First: God protects both believers and nonbelievers. His mercy does not depend on our faith, although our faith helps us recognize His hand.

Second: God often works through obedient people. Miracles happen when someone is willing to look foolish in the eyes of the world in order to obey God's voice.

Third: Moments of divine protection can be spiritual turning points. What begins as physical salvation can lead to spiritual salvation.

Fourth: Learning to hear God's voice can literally save lives
—our own and others'.

The Multiplied Testimony

Miguel became a walking testimony to God's protective power. At his company, he shared the story with colleagues. At family gatherings, he told how God had saved his family.

"I used to mock religious people," he said openly. "I thought they were ignorant or naive. But now I know—there is a God who cares enough to wake up a neighbor at three in the morning to save a family of skeptics."

His story impacted dozens of people who also considered themselves "too skeptical" or "too smart" for faith. If God could reach Miguel—the pragmatic, skeptical, business-minded man
who only believed in what he could see and measure—perhaps He could reach anyone.

Perpetual Gratitude

Years later, every time Miguel saw Ceulemans, his gratitude was palpable.

"You saved my family," he would always say.

And Ceulemans would always correct him: "It wasn't me. It was God. I just obeyed."

"Yes," Miguel would agree. "But you obeyed. And your obedience saved five lives that night. How can I ever thank you enough?"

"Live a life that honors the one who saved you," Ceulemans replied. "That is the best gratitude."

And Miguel did just that—he lived each day with the awareness that it had been given to him as a gift, not a guarantee. Every moment with his children was precious because he knew how close he had come to losing them forever.

"God's protection is real, present, and personal."

CHAPTER 10: THE LOST SON

"God desires family unity and reconciliation" (Luke 24:52)

The Broken Mother

Mrs. Teresa entered the small office where Ceulemans saw people for spiritual counseling. She was about 65 years old, with gray hair and eyes that carried the weight of years of unresolved pain.

"I don't know where to start," she said, her voice trembling. "It's been so long that I don't even know if there's any hope."

Ceulemans pointed to the comfortable chair. "Start at the beginning. God has given us all the time we need."

Teresa took a deep breath. "My son. I haven't spoken to him in fifteen years. Fifteen years since he left home and said he never wanted to see me again."

Tears began to fall. "I don't even know where he lives. If he's alive. If he's happy. I've lost fifteen years of my son's life."

The Old Story

The story was painful and complicated, as so many family stories are. Teresa had been a single mother, raising Daniel alone after their father abandoned them when the boy was only three years old.

"I worked three jobs to give him everything he needed," she explained. "Private school, nice clothes, food on the table. I sacrificed myself for him." But Daniel, growing up without a father and with a mother who was always absent because of work, developed resentment. As a teenager, he became rebellious. They fought constantly.

"The last fight was terrible," Teresa recalled, the pain still fresh after fifteen years. "He was 22. He wanted to drop out of college to join a band. I told him he was throwing his life away, that I hadn't worked so hard to see him waste opportunities."

"He told me I was never really there for him, that all I cared about was appearances and success. He said I was controlling and that he hated me." Her voice broke. "Then he packed his things and left. And he never came back."

The Failed Attempt

"I tried to contact him at first," Teresa continued. "I called, I sent messages. He blocked my number. I went to his house, he didn't open the door. After a few months, he moved and didn't leave a new address."

"Eventually, I stopped trying. I thought that if he wanted me out of his life, I should respect that. But not a day goes by without me thinking about him. Without wondering where I went wrong."

As she spoke, Ceulemans prayed silently. And the Holy Spirit began to reveal things that Teresa had not said.

"Teresa," he said gently, "you're not telling me everything. There's more to the story of the last fight, isn't there?"

She turned pale. "How did you...?"
"Tell me what really happened," Ceulemans encouraged her.

The Hidden Truth

Teresa cried harder now, years of guilt finally finding voice. "When he said he hated me, I... I said that sometimes I wished I had never had a child. That my life would have been easier without him."

She covered her face with her hands. "I didn't mean it. I was angry, hurt. But the words came out. And I saw something die in his eyes at that moment."

"He said, 'Finally, the truth,' and left. And I never had a chance to say it wasn't true, that I said it out of anger, that he's the most important thing in my life."

"That guilt has consumed you for fifteen years," Ceulemans said. It wasn't a question.

"Every day," she whispered. "How does a mother say that to her son? What kind of monster am I?"

The Divine Revelation

"Teresa," Ceulemans said, feeling the Holy Spirit guiding his words, "your son is alive and living just two hours from here."

She stared at him with wide eyes. "How could you know that?"

"He also carries pain," Ceulemans continued. "He got married five years ago. He has a three-year-old daughter. And every time he looks at her, he thinks of you. He wants reconciliation as much as you do, but he's afraid of being rejected."

"How do you know these things?" Teresa asked, between hope and disbelief.

"God showed me," Ceulemans replied simply. "And what's more, he'll be at a specific café in three days, on Wednesday, at noon. A café called 'Café Aurora' in the city center."

Teresa was trembling. "Should I go? What if he doesn't want to see me? What if he still hates me?"

The Preparation

Over the next three days, Ceulemans met with Teresa daily, preparing her for the encounter.

"You need to be ready to ask for forgiveness without expectations," he explained. "Don't go expecting him to forgive you immediately. Go prepared to simply tell your truth and leave the rest to God."

They practiced what she would say. They prayed for Daniel's heart to be opened. They worked through Teresa's guilt, helping her accept that although she had made a terrible mistake, she was not defined by that moment.

"God can restore what the enemy has stolen," Ceulemans encouraged her. "Fifteen lost years cannot be recovered, but the future can still be redeemed."

The Encounter

At noon on Wednesday, Teresa walked into Café Aurora with her heart pounding so hard she thought everyone could hear it. And there, sitting at a table by the window, was Daniel.

He was older, of course. He was no longer the 22-year-old who had stormed out. He was 37 now, with a few wrinkles around his eyes, but still recognizable as the boy she had raised.

When he saw her, he froze. His face went through a series of expressions— shock, anger, pain, confusion.

Teresa approached slowly. "Daniel," she said, her voice barely more than a whisper. "Please don't leave. I just need five minutes."

He didn't answer, but he didn't get up to leave either. She took that as permission to sit down.

The Long-Awaited Words

"I've rehearsed this a thousand times over the last three days," Teresa began, tears already streaming down her face. "But now that you're here, all I can say is: forgive me."

"Those words I said that day—that I wished I'd never had a child—were the biggest lie I've ever told. And the worst thing I ever did was let you believe them."

"You are the best gift I have ever received," she continued. "Every sacrifice I made, I made gladly because it was for you. I made many mistakes. I worked too hard, I was absent too often, I was too controlling. But never, not for a second, did I stop loving you more than my own life."

Daniel stood motionless, his eyes glistening with unshed tears.
"I don't expect you to forgive me," Teresa said. "I don't deserve forgiveness. But I needed you to know the truth. And if you'll allow me, I'd like to meet my granddaughter. Not to interfere, not to control. Just to be there in the way I couldn't be for you."

The Answer

The silence that followed seemed to last an eternity. Then Daniel spoke, his voice hoarse with emotion.

"How did you know I would be here?" he asked.

"A man named Ceulemans told me," Teresa replied. "He said God showed him where you would be."

Daniel turned pale. "Ceulemans? Dark hair, maybe 45 years old?" "Yes, do you

know him?"

"He came up to me a week ago," Daniel said, still processing. "He stopped in the parking lot where I was and started talking to me. He said my mother loved me and that I needed to forgive her. He said there would be an opportunity for reconciliation."

"I thought he was crazy," Daniel admitted. "But there was something about the way he spoke... And then he told me he'd be at this café today, at this exact time."

"He set us both up," Teresa realized, amazed.

The Break

"Mom," Daniel said, and hearing that word again after fifteen years broke something in Teresa. "I also need to ask for forgiveness. I
was cruel. I said horrible things. And when you tried to reconcile in the first few months, I rejected every attempt. My pride wouldn't let me forgive."

"I got married, had a daughter, and discovered that being a father is the hardest and most important thing in the world. And I finally understood how much you sacrificed for me. How many mistakes I will probably make too."

"Every birthday, every Christmas, I wanted to call," he confessed. "But I was ashamed. So much time had passed. How could I just come back?"

They cried together, years of pain finally finding release. Other customers in the café discreetly looked away, giving them privacy in their moment.

The Restoration

That afternoon, Daniel took Teresa to meet his granddaughter, Sofia. The three-year-old girl looked at the stranger with curiosity.

"Sofia," Daniel said, kneeling beside his daughter, "this is your grandmother. Daddy's mother."

"I have a grandmother?" Sofia's eyes widened.

"You always have," Daniel said, looking at his mother. "We just hadn't seen her in a long time. But now she's here."

Sofia, with the simplicity of children, simply stretched out her arms. "Hi, Grandma!"

And when Teresa held her granddaughter in her arms for the first time, she felt fifteen years of pain replaced by hope. The

past couldn't be changed, but the future was open and bright.

The Healing Process

Reconciliation was not instantaneous or perfect. There were uncomfortable moments, old wounds that still hurt, patterns that needed to be broken.

Teresa had to learn not to be controlling, to offer her opinion only when asked, to trust Daniel's choices as a father. Daniel had to work through old resentments that occasionally resurfaced.

But they persevered. Family dinners began as monthly events, then became weekly. Sofia filled their lives with joy and laughter, serving as the bridge that connected the past and the future.

"Children are gifts from God in many ways," Teresa told Ceulemans months later. "Sofia didn't just give me a second chance at being a grandmother. She gave me a second chance with my son."

The Greater Lesson

Teresa and Daniel's story taught profound truths about family and forgiveness:

First: It is never too late for reconciliation. Fifteen years is a long time, but it is not too late when God is involved.

Second: Pride and shame keep families apart. Both sides wanted reconciliation, but fear prevented the first step.

Third: God can orchestrate encounters that seem impossible. Divine timing put mother and son in the same place at the right moment.

Fourth: Forgiveness is a process, not a single event. Real reconciliation requires ongoing work and daily choices of grace.

The Living Testimony

When asked how reconciliation happened, Teresa and Daniel always told about Ceulemans—the man God used to bring a broken family together.

"He came to us separately," Daniel explained. "He prepared our hearts. And then He put us in the same place at the right time."

"It was as if God said, 'Enough separation,'" Teresa added. "And He sent His messenger to bring us back together."

Years later, when Sofia was ten and asked why she didn't know her grandmother when she was a baby, Daniel told her the whole story— the mistakes, the separation, the pride, and finally the reconciliation.

"And that," he concluded, "is why we never let the sun go down on our anger. Why we always apologize when we're wrong. Because we learned the hard way how much time can be lost to pride."

"Restored family—the desire of God's heart."

CHAPTER 11: PROSPERITY WITH PURPOSE

"God prospers His people for greater purposes" (Genesis 1:28)

The Family in Crisis

Lucia knocked on Ceulemans' office door hesitantly. She was embarrassed to be there, to have to ask for help. But she had run out of options.

"I don't know if you can help me," she said, barely able to make eye contact. "My problem isn't spiritual. It's financial."

"Come in," Ceulemans said gently. "Let's talk."

Lucia was 42 years old, the mother of two teenage children. Her husband had died two years earlier of a sudden heart attack, leaving her alone with a mountain of medical bills and insufficient life insurance.

"I'm three months behind on rent," she confessed, the words coming out with difficulty. "The landlord is going to evict us next week. I have two jobs, but it's not enough. The medical bills... they never stop coming."

She paused, wiping away tears. "My kids don't deserve this. They already lost their father. Now they're going to lose their home too."

The Unexpected Question

Ceulemans listened to the whole story—the debts, the jobs that barely covered the basics, the impossible choices between food and medicine.

Then he asked a question that took her by surprise. "Lucia, when was the last time you gave something to someone?"

She blinked, confused. "What do you mean? I have nothing to give. I'm literally about to be evicted."

"I understand," Ceulemans said. "But answer the question. When was the last time you gave anything—time, money, help
—to someone in need?"

Lucia thought. "I don't know. Years ago, I think. Before my husband died. Now I'm the one who needs help, not the one who helps."

"And that's exactly where the problem lies," Ceulemans said gently.

The Reverse Principle

"What you're about to tell me is going to sound crazy," Ceulemans continued. "But it's been working for thousands of years, and it will work for you too."

He opened his Bible. "The principle of sowing and reaping. You can't reap what you don't plant. And when you're in scarcity, the last thing your instinct tells you to do is give. But that's exactly what God asks you to do."

"You want me to give money I don't have?" Lucia asked incredulously.

"I want you to give something—whatever you can. Not because it will magically solve your problems, but because it changes your mindset from scarcity to trust. It tells God, 'I trust You to provide.'"

Lucia was skeptical. "That sounds like those television preachers who just want money."

"I'm not asking you to give me anything," Ceulemans clarified. "I'm telling you to find someone in need and help
— even if it's something small. And watch what God does."

The First Step

Lucia left the conversation feeling uncomfortable. How could she give when she was about to lose everything? But something in Ceulemans' words stayed with her.

A few days later, at the supermarket buying the bare minimum with her last twenty dollars, she saw an elderly woman counting coins at the checkout, clearly without enough money for her groceries.

The voice in her head said, "You need that money. You have children to feed." But a softer voice whispered, "Trust Me."

Before she could overthink it, Lucia approached. "Let me cover this," she said, her hand trembling as she handed over ten dollars—half of what she had.

The lady looked at her with tears in her eyes. "God bless you, child."

Lucia walked out of the market feeling strange—part of her panicked that she had given away half her money, part of her at peace in a way she didn't understand.

The Unexpected Change

Two days later, Lucia received a call from an unknown number.
"Ms. Lucia Martinez?" The voice was professional. "This is the law firm of Thompson & Associates. We've been trying to reach you for months."

Her heart sank. More debt? More problems?

"Your late husband had a life insurance policy through a previous job that was not listed in his primary documents. We just located it through our audit process. The amount is $150,000."

Lucia had to sit down. "What? That's not possible."

"Yes, ma'am. The process will take a few weeks, but the money is legally yours."

The Reaction

Lucia rushed to Ceulemans' house, almost unable to breathe. "You won't believe what happened!"

She told him about the call, about the lost insurance policy that no one knew existed, about how it would pay off all her debts and still have money left over.

"Was it because of the ten dollars?" she asked. "Giving those ten dollars made this happen?"

"Not exactly," Ceulemans explained. "That insurance always existed. But your act of giving, of trusting despite scarcity, opened your spiritual eyes to see God's provision. And God chose that moment to reveal what was already there."

"But there is something important," he continued seriously. "This money is not just for you. It is for a purpose."

The Greater Purpose

In the weeks that followed, as the insurance process moved forward, Ceulemans met regularly with Lucia, teaching her about financial stewardship.

"God didn't give you this money just to save you," he explained. "He gave it to you so that you can be a blessing to others."

Together, they came up with a plan. Pay off all the debts first. Establish an emergency fund. And then, use a significant portion to help others.

"But I need that money," Lucia argued. "My children need to go to college."

"And they will," Ceulemans assured her. "But if you keep it all for yourself, you'll miss out on the multiplied blessing that comes from giving. God tested you with ten dollars at the grocery store. Now He's testing you with $150,000."

70

The Decision

Lucia wrestled with the decision. The part of her that had lived in scarcity wanted to hold on to every penny. But a new part of her, one that was learning to trust, knew Ceulemans was right.

She decided to donate 20%—$30,000—to various causes. She paid off medical bills for families she knew who were struggling. She gave to the church. She established a scholarship fund for children of widowed parents.

"Every time I give," she said in wonder, "I feel like I'm getting more back. Not in money, but in peace, in joy, in purpose."

The Multiplication

In the months that followed, something extraordinary happened. Lucia, now financially stable, began to see opportunities everywhere.

A friend mentioned an investment property. With careful guidance and prayer, she invested. The value doubled in a year.

She started a small business baking cakes—something she had always loved but never had time for. The business grew rapidly through word of mouth.

"It doesn't make sense," she told Ceulemans. "I should just be keeping my head above water. Instead, I'm thriving."

"It makes sense when you understand God's principles," Ceulemans replied. "When you give generously and manage faithfully what God gives you, He entrusts more to you."

The Test

Two years after receiving the insurance money, Lucia was in a financial situation she had never imagined. Her children had college funds. She owned her own home. Her cake business had three employees.

Then came the test. Her sister, who had always been irresponsible with money, called needing $20,000 to keep her business from going bankrupt.

Lucia struggled. Giving to strangers was one thing. But giving to someone whose mismanagement had created her own crisis?

"What do I do?" she asked Ceulemans.
"What does your heart say?" he replied.

"My heart says give. My head says it's foolish." "Then you already know the

answer," Ceulemans smiled.

Lucia gave her sister the money, but with conditions—financial counseling, accountability, a clear plan. To her surprise, her sister accepted all the conditions.

The Complete Transformation

Three years after that first conversation in Ceulemans' office, Lucia was a totally different person. Not just financially, but in her whole approach to life.

"I used to live with a scarcity mindset," she reflected. "Always worried that there wouldn't be enough. Always holding on tight. But God taught me that the more I let go, the more He can give me."

Her cake business now employed eight people, all single mothers who needed flexible work. "I remember what it was like," Lucia explained. "So I created the kind of job I would have liked to have had."

She also started a support group for widows, teaching financial planning and faith. "The financial part is important," she said. "But the faith part is what really changes everything."

The Profound Lesson

Lucia's story taught important truths about prosperity and purpose:
First: God prospers people not only for their comfort, but to expand their capacity to bless others.

Second: Generosity in scarcity opens doors that greed in abundance closes.

Third: True prosperity is not just about having money, but about having purpose and peace.

Fourth: What seems like sacrifice in giving often returns multiplied in unexpected ways.

The Living Testimony

When people asked Lucia the secret of her financial transformation, she always told the whole story—the scarcity, the ten dollars at the grocery store, the uncovered insurance, and the journey of learning to give.

"It wasn't magic," she explained. "It was spiritual principle. God was waiting for me to trust Him enough to open my hand, even when it seemed I had nothing to give."

Dozens of people were inspired by her story. Some began to give even in their own difficulties and saw similar changes. Others learned to manage what they had more wisely.

And Lucia? She continued to prosper, not because she accumulated, but because she continued to give. Each year, she increased her donations. Each year, God seemed to open new doors.

"Purposeful prosperity," she often said, "is not about how much you have. It's about how much you can give and still trust that God will provide more."

"True prosperity is having enough for your needs and generosity for the needs of others."

CHAPTER 12: THE POWER THAT COMES FROM ABOVE

"Every person has access to divine guidance and purpose" (Colossians 1:16)

The Complete Journey

Sitting on his porch at sunset, Ceulemans reflected on the extraordinary journey God had taken him on. From a 21-year-old lost on the streets of Boston to an instrument through which the Holy Spirit touched lives in ways he could never have imagined.

He thought of all the people he had met along the way. The lady at the supermarket who didn't have money for her groceries. The young man collecting carts in the parking lot. The family at Disney whose daughter was healed. Roberto and Marcela whose marriage was restored. Patricia who found her true calling. Carlos freed from addiction. Miguel saved from the gas leak. Teresa and Daniel reconciled. Lucia who learned prosperity with purpose.

Each story was unique, but they all shared a common thread: the power of God working through an obedient heart.

The Pattern Revealed

"It wasn't about me," Ceulemans murmured to himself. It was a truth he had learned repeatedly over the years. Every miracle, every transformation, every moment of divine intervention—none of it happened because of his own strength, wisdom, or holiness.

He was simply an available vessel. Someone who had learned to recognize God's voice and had chosen to obey, even when it didn't make sense, even when it was inconvenient, even when it risked looking foolish.

The pattern was always the same: God spoke, he obeyed, miracles happened, lives were transformed, and God received all the glory.

The Universal Question

But as he reflected, Ceulemans knew that the question many would have was simple: "How can I hear God's voice like you do?"

It was the question he was asked constantly. People who wanted to experience what he experienced, who wanted to be used by God the way he was used.

And his answer was always the same: "You already can. God speaks to everyone. The question is not whether He is speaking, but whether we are listening."

Recognizing the Voice

Over the years, Ceulemans had learned to recognize God's voice in various ways:

Sometimes it was a soft whisper in his spirit, an impression that did not come from his own thoughts. Other times it was an urgency that woke him from sleep, as on the night he was alerted to Miguel's gas leak.

Sometimes it came through Scripture, where a passage he had read dozens of times suddenly took on new meaning for
a specific situation. Other times it was through dreams or visions, as when he saw where Daniel would be to meet his mother.

But the common denominator was always peace. God's voice brought peace, even when He asked for difficult things. The voices of doubt, fear, or pride brought anxiety and confusion.

The Practical Principles

For those who wanted to develop this spiritual sensitivity, Ceulemans always shared some practical principles he had learned:

First: Cultivate silence. In the modern world full of constant noise, God often speaks in silence. Set aside time each day just to sit in quiet, without your phone, without distractions, and simply be present with God.

Second: Know the Scriptures. God will never say anything that contradicts His written word. The more you know the Bible, the more easily you will recognize His voice.

Third: Start with small acts of obedience. Before God entrusts you with big tasks, He tests your faithfulness in small ones. If you feel impressed to encourage someone, do an act of kindness, or give something—obey. These small acts of obedience train your spiritual sensitivity.

Fourth: Wait for confirmation. Especially for big decisions, God often confirms through multiple sources—Scripture, circumstances, wise counsel from other believers, and persistent inner peace.

Fifth: Don't fear error. You will sometimes confuse your own thoughts with God's voice. That's part of learning. God is patient with our honest mistakes as we learn to listen to Him.

The Individual Purpose

"But I'm not special like you," people often said to Ceulemans. And he always laughed.

"I'm not special," he would reply. "I'm simply obedient. And you can be too."

The truth he had discovered was revolutionary: God has no favorites. He does not reserve His voice and power for only a select few. Every person born has a divine purpose, a unique calling, and direct access to the Holy Spirit.

The problem was never that God wasn't speaking. The problem was that people weren't listening, or they listened but chose not to obey.

Your Own Holy Ground

"Sacred Ground is not a place," Ceulemans often taught. "It is a state of being. It is anywhere you encounter God and obey His voice."

For him, it had been the streets of Boston where he got lost and learned to trust divine guidance. It had been a supermarket where he helped an elderly lady. It had been Disney where a little girl was healed.

But for you, reader, your Sacred Ground will be different. It may be your workplace, where God calls you to show integrity and
love. It may be your home, where you are called to be a peacemaker and intercessor. It may be a street corner where you meet someone in need.

Sacred Ground is not about geography—it is about availability. It is about being willing to be used by God wherever you are.

The Challenge

If you have come this far on this journey, Ceulemans had a challenge for you:

Stop reading for a moment. Close your eyes. And ask God, "Why did you create me? What is my purpose?"

Don't expect an audible voice. Don't expect a dramatic vision. But pay attention to the impressions that come. To the thoughts that linger. To the passions that stir in your heart.

God planted seeds of purpose in you even before you were born. He placed gifts, talents, passions, and callings within you. The question is not whether they exist—it's whether you are willing to discover them and walk in them.

The Daily Decision

"Living on Sacred Ground is a daily decision," Ceulemans explained. "It's not a destination you reach and then relax. It's a choice you make every morning when you wake up."

The choice to listen rather than simply pray. The choice to obey rather than rationalize. The choice to trust rather than control. The choice to give rather than accumulate. The choice to serve rather than be served.

These daily choices, accumulated over months and years, transform an ordinary life into an extraordinary journey of faith and impact.

The Final Invitation

As the sun set, painting the sky with shades of orange and pink, Ceulemans felt the Holy Spirit impressing a final message on his heart— not for him, but for you:

"You were created for more than just to exist. You were created with divine purpose. There are people only you can reach. There is work only you can do. There is a role only you can fill in God's great plan."

"The world is full of need. Broken hearts need healing. Divided families need reconciliation. Lost souls need direction. And God wants to use you—yes, you—to make a difference."

"You don't need special credentials. You don't need formal theological training. You don't need to be perfect. You just need to be available."

The Promise

"And here's the promise," Ceulemans continued, as if speaking directly to each reader, "when you say yes to God, when you choose to walk in obedience, He commits to equip you, guide you, and sustain you."

"You will never be alone. The same Holy Spirit who guided a lost young immigrant in Boston is available to you. The same power that healed a girl at

Disney is available to
you. The same wisdom that restored marriages and freed addicts is available
to you."

"The power that comes from above is not reserved for a select few. It is the
inheritance of every son and daughter of God."

The Beginning

"This is not the conclusion of a story," Ceulemans smiled, watching the first
stars appear in the dark sky. "It is the beginning of yours."

"Each chapter you've read wasn't just about my journey. It was a mirror
showing possibilities for your own journey. Where you see God working in my
life, know that He desires to work in yours as well."

"Sacred Ground is waiting for you. Not in some distant place you need to
travel to find, but right where you are now. Your home can be Sacred Ground.
Your job can be Sacred Ground. Your neighborhood can be Sacred Ground."

"The only question is: are you ready to step into it with faith?"

The Final Prayer

Ceulemans closed his eyes and prayed, not only for himself, but for every
person who would read these words:

"Father, for every person who has come this far, I pray that You will awaken
within them a hunger for Your purpose. That You will open their spiritual ears
to hear Your voice. That You will give them courage to obey even when it
doesn't make sense."

"May they discover their own Sacred Grounds, those places and moments
where You meet them in personal and powerful ways."

"And may their lives become living testimonies of Your power, love, and faithfulness. Not so that they may be celebrated, but so that You may be glorified."

"Use them, Lord. Each one of them. For purposes only You know. Amen."

The End That Is a Beginning

As Ceulemans got up to go inside, he knew the story would continue. Not through him alone, but through every person who chose to respond to God's call.

Through you.

The journey of Sacred Ground does not end with the last page of this book. It begins when you close the book and choose to live what you have learned.

When you choose to listen. To obey. To trust. To give. To serve.

When you choose to be a vessel through which the power that comes from above can flow into a world in need.

Your Sacred Ground is waiting. What will you do?

"The end of a story, the beginning of your journey."

Visiting a Church

"My wife and I at the time, she was my girlfriend, her name was Verônica Cristina, 11 years ago, in a Christian church, very humble but with the presence of the Holy Spirit transforming, a new church.

She had already visited before. As we were starting our relationship, she wanted to start our life the right way, between the paths of our lives with the Lord Jesus Christ, not running away from church or work in the church. This pastor knew her because she was a woman named Toninha, she was the one who preached the word of God that night, a life-transforming experience that I will never forget."

The words that came out of her mouth were, my son. God has a purpose for your life, He is giving you the keys of heaven to walk in His presence. He will do everything your heart desires. God wants you whole, He is saying that He doesn't want reservation, He wants you entirely.

When she began to speak these words, it came from heaven. I couldn't resist, I knelt down, and the words that were manifested at that moment were impactful. It came like an arrow to my heart and spoke to my soul. I was moving, and many people were impacted by the presence of God, especially by the word of God. This is the power of the word of God."

"They were impacted by the presence of God. The songs that were sung were speaking to my heart, everything was happening as if someone had told all my life to the people.

I began to speak internally, 'My God, how is this happening? What will happen until the end of this service?' My hands were shaking, and my heart was racing, my eyes tearing up. If I looked, the tears were writing and without realizing it, the one who was next to me was my girlfriend, and she didn't want to surprise me, but she started crying too, and almost at the end of the service, she called me and said, 'I knew that this was something from God.' I was convinced that God was using her to transform my life.

EPILOGUE

Years later, when people asked Ceulemans about his greatest legacy, he always answered the same way:

"It's not the stories I told or the people I helped. My greatest legacy is those who heard the call and chose to respond. Those who discovered that they too could hear God's voice and be used by Him."

"Because when a person finds their purpose and walks in it, they touch dozens of other lives. And those people touch hundreds. And the impact continues to multiply until the kingdom of God expands in ways we could never count or measure."

"That's the beauty of Embracing Divine Purpose. It's not just my story. It's our story. And the story never really ends—it just finds new chapters in new lives."

END